This
DAILY GRATITUDE JOURNAL
belongs to:

....

Daily Gratitude Journal

FOR KIDS

PETER PAUPER PRESS, INC.

WHITE PLAINS, NEW YORK

PETER PAUPER PRESS

In 1928, at the age of twenty-two, Peter Beilenson began printing books on a small press in the basement of his parents' home in Larchmont, New York. Peter—and later, his wife, Edna—sought to create fine books that sold at "prices even a pauper could afford."

Today, still family owned and operated, Peter Pauper Press continues to honor our founders' legacy of quality, value, and fun for big kids and small kids alike.

Cover illustration courtesy of Creative Market
Designed by Heather Zschock

Copyright © 2022
Peter Pauper Press, Inc.
202 Mamaroneck Avenue
White Plains, NY 10601 USA
All rights reserved
ISBN 978-1-4413-3821-1
Printed in China
7 6 5 4 3 2 1

Visit us at www.peterpauper.com

Gratitude paints smiley faces
on everything it touches.

— RICHELLE E. GOODRICH

Let this journal guide the way to cultivating an attitude of gratitude. Making time each day to express gratitude can help your child feel happier and more self-confident. Daily prompts encourage your child to focus on what they are thankful for, how they feel, and what has made them happy.

At the end of each week, space is provided to write about how they put gratitude into action through acts of kindness. The possibilities are endless and entirely up to your child. Gratitude in Action at the end of this journal offers suggestions. This practice provides a wonderful way to spend time together and reflect on the positives of each day.

Grateful to
Be Me

My Self-Portrait:

MY NAME HERE

Things I love about myself:

People I am grateful for:

My favorite places:

Foods I love:

The BEST part of school:

Activities I enjoy:

Be yourself, and people will like you.

– JEFF KINNEY, *DIARY OF A WIMPY KID*

Date:

Today I am thankful for:

Someone I am grateful to:

How I feel:

☐ HAPPY ☐ SAD ☐ EXCITED ☐ CALM ☐ GROUCHY ☐ _____
OTHER

The BEST part of my day (draw and/or write about it):

Date: ....

Today I am thankful for: ....

....

....

....

....

Someone I am grateful to: ....

....

....

How I feel:

☐ HAPPY   ☐ SAD   ☐ EXCITED   ☐ CALM   ☐ GROUCHY   ☐ _____
                                                        OTHER

The BEST part of my day (draw and/or write about it):

Date:

Today I am thankful for:

Someone I am grateful to:

How I feel:

☐ HAPPY   ☐ SAD   ☐ EXCITED   ☐ CALM   ☐ GROUCHY   ☐ _____
OTHER

The **BEST** part of my day (draw and/or write about it):

Date:

Today I am thankful for:

Someone I am grateful to:

How I feel:

☐ HAPPY ☐ SAD ☐ EXCITED ☐ CALM ☐ GROUCHY ☐ _____
OTHER

The **BEST** part of my day (draw and/or write about it):

Date:

Today I am thankful for:

Someone I am grateful to:

How I feel:

☐ HAPPY ☐ SAD ☐ EXCITED ☐ CALM ☐ GROUCHY ☐ _____
OTHER

The BEST part of my day (draw and/or write about it):

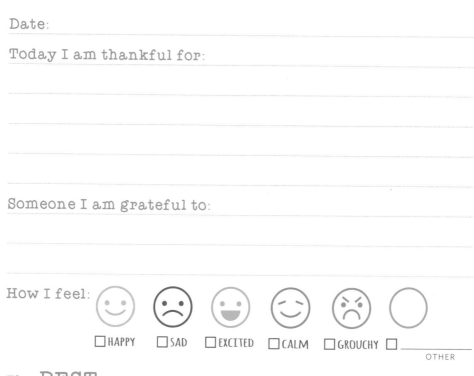

Date:

Today I am thankful for:

Someone I am grateful to:

How I feel:

☐ HAPPY   ☐ SAD   ☐ EXCITED   ☐ CALM   ☐ GROUCHY   ☐ _____
OTHER

The BEST part of my day (draw and/or write about it):

Date: _____

Today I am thankful for: _____

_____

_____

_____

Someone I am grateful to: _____

_____

How I feel: ☺ ☹ 😃 ☺ 😠 ◯

☐ HAPPY   ☐ SAD   ☐ EXCITED   ☐ CALM   ☐ GROUCHY   ☐ _____
                                                          OTHER

The **BEST** part of my day (draw and/or write about it):

Weekly Acts of Kindness

How I showed kindness this week:

_____

_____

_____

_____

_____

What I'm looking forward to next week:

_____

_____

_____

_____

_____

I am beginning to learn it is the
sweet simple things of life which
are the real ones after all.

– LAURA INGALLS WILDER

Date:

Today I am thankful for:

Someone I am grateful to:

How I feel:

☐ HAPPY ☐ SAD ☐ EXCITED ☐ CALM ☐ GROUCHY ☐ _____
                                                          OTHER

The BEST part of my day (draw and/or write about it):

Date:

Today I am thankful for:

Someone I am grateful to:

How I feel:

☐ HAPPY ☐ SAD ☐ EXCITED ☐ CALM ☐ GROUCHY ☐ _____
OTHER

The BEST part of my day (draw and/or write about it):

Date:

Today I am thankful for:

Someone I am grateful to:

How I feel:

☐ HAPPY ☐ SAD ☐ EXCITED ☐ CALM ☐ GROUCHY ☐ _____
OTHER

The BEST part of my day (draw and/or write about it):

Date:

Today I am thankful for:

Someone I am grateful to:

How I feel:

☐ HAPPY ☐ SAD ☐ EXCITED ☐ CALM ☐ GROUCHY ☐ _____
OTHER

The BEST part of my day (draw and/or write about it):

Date:

Today I am thankful for:

Someone I am grateful to:

How I feel:

☐ HAPPY   ☐ SAD   ☐ EXCITED   ☐ CALM   ☐ GROUCHY   ☐ _____
                                                              OTHER

The BEST part of my day (draw and/or write about it):

Date:

Today I am thankful for:

Someone I am grateful to:

How I feel:

☐ HAPPY ☐ SAD ☐ EXCITED ☐ CALM ☐ GROUCHY ☐ _____
OTHER

The BEST part of my day (draw and/or write about it):

Date: ....

Today I am thankful for: ....

....

....

....

....

Someone I am grateful to: ....

....

....

How I feel:

☐ HAPPY ☐ SAD ☐ EXCITED ☐ CALM ☐ GROUCHY ☐ _____
OTHER

The **BEST** part of my day (draw and/or write about it):

Weekly Acts of Kindness

How I showed kindness this week:

_____

_____

_____

_____

_____

What I'm looking forward to next week:

_____

_____

_____

_____

_____

There are flowers everywhere for
those who want to see them.

– HENRI MATISSE

Date:

Today I am thankful for:

Someone I am grateful to:

How I feel:

☐ HAPPY   ☐ SAD   ☐ EXCITED   ☐ CALM   ☐ GROUCHY   ☐ _____
OTHER

The BEST part of my day (draw and/or write about it):

Date:

Today I am thankful for:

Someone I am grateful to:

How I feel:

☐ HAPPY   ☐ SAD   ☐ EXCITED   ☐ CALM   ☐ GROUCHY   ☐ _____
OTHER

The **BEST** part of my day (draw and/or write about it):

Date:

Today I am thankful for:

Someone I am grateful to:

How I feel:

☐ HAPPY   ☐ SAD   ☐ EXCITED   ☐ CALM   ☐ GROUCHY   ☐ _____
OTHER

The **BEST** part of my day (draw and/or write about it):

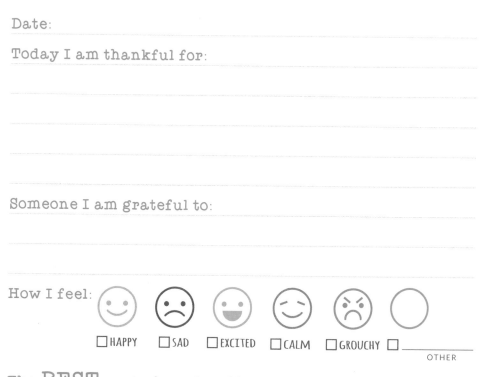

Date: _____

Today I am thankful for:

_____

_____

_____

_____

Someone I am grateful to:

_____

_____

How I feel:
☐ HAPPY ☐ SAD ☐ EXCITED ☐ CALM ☐ GROUCHY ☐ _____
OTHER

The BEST part of my day (draw and/or write about it):

Date:

Today I am thankful for:

Someone I am grateful to:

How I feel:

☐ HAPPY ☐ SAD ☐ EXCITED ☐ CALM ☐ GROUCHY ☐ _____
                                                              OTHER

The **BEST** part of my day (draw and/or write about it):

Date:

Today I am thankful for:

Someone I am grateful to:

How I feel:

☐ HAPPY ☐ SAD ☐ EXCITED ☐ CALM ☐ GROUCHY ☐ _____
OTHER

The BEST part of my day (draw and/or write about it):

Date:

Today I am thankful for:

Someone I am grateful to:

How I feel:

☐ HAPPY ☐ SAD ☐ EXCITED ☐ CALM ☐ GROUCHY ☐ _____
OTHER

The BEST part of my day (draw and/or write about it):

Weekly Acts of
Kindness

How I showed kindness this week:

_____

_____

_____

_____

_____

What I'm looking forward to next week:

_____

_____

_____

_____

_____

You have been my friend.
That in itself is a tremendous thing.

– E. B. WHITE, *CHARLOTTE'S WEB*

Date:

Today I am thankful for:

Someone I am grateful to:

How I feel:

☐ HAPPY   ☐ SAD   ☐ EXCITED   ☐ CALM   ☐ GROUCHY   ☐ _____
OTHER

The BEST part of my day (draw and/or write about it):

Date:

Today I am thankful for:

Someone I am grateful to:

How I feel:

☐ HAPPY ☐ SAD ☐ EXCITED ☐ CALM ☐ GROUCHY ☐ _____
OTHER

The BEST part of my day (draw and/or write about it):

Date: ....

Today I am thankful for: ....

....

....

....

....

Someone I am grateful to: ....

....

....

How I feel:

☐ HAPPY ☐ SAD ☐ EXCITED ☐ CALM ☐ GROUCHY ☐ _____
OTHER

The BEST part of my day (draw and/or write about it):

Date:

Today I am thankful for:

Someone I am grateful to:

How I feel:

☐ HAPPY ☐ SAD ☐ EXCITED ☐ CALM ☐ GROUCHY ☐ _____
OTHER

The BEST part of my day (draw and/or write about it):

Date:

Today I am thankful for:

Someone I am grateful to:

How I feel: ☺ ☹ 😃 ☺ 😠 ◯

☐ HAPPY ☐ SAD ☐ EXCITED ☐ CALM ☐ GROUCHY ☐ _____ OTHER

The BEST part of my day (draw and/or write about it):

Date:

Today I am thankful for:

Someone I am grateful to:

How I feel:

☐ HAPPY ☐ SAD ☐ EXCITED ☐ CALM ☐ GROUCHY ☐ _____
OTHER

The **BEST** part of my day (draw and/or write about it):

Date:

Today I am thankful for:

Someone I am grateful to:

How I feel:

☐ HAPPY ☐ SAD ☐ EXCITED ☐ CALM ☐ GROUCHY ☐ _____
OTHER

The BEST part of my day (draw and/or write about it):

Weekly Acts of Kindness

How I showed kindness this week:

What I'm looking forward to next week:

Find the good and praise it.

— ALEX HALEY

Date:

Today I am thankful for:

Someone I am grateful to:

How I feel:

☐ HAPPY ☐ SAD ☐ EXCITED ☐ CALM ☐ GROUCHY ☐ _____
OTHER

The BEST part of my day (draw and/or write about it):

Date:

Today I am thankful for:

Someone I am grateful to:

How I feel:

☐ HAPPY ☐ SAD ☐ EXCITED ☐ CALM ☐ GROUCHY ☐ _____
OTHER

The **BEST** part of my day (draw and/or write about it):

Date:

Today I am thankful for:

Someone I am grateful to:

How I feel:

☐ HAPPY ☐ SAD ☐ EXCITED ☐ CALM ☐ GROUCHY ☐ _____ OTHER

The BEST part of my day (draw and/or write about it):

Date:

Today I am thankful for:

Someone I am grateful to:

How I feel:

☐ HAPPY ☐ SAD ☐ EXCITED ☐ CALM ☐ GROUCHY ☐ _____
OTHER

The BEST part of my day (draw and/or write about it):

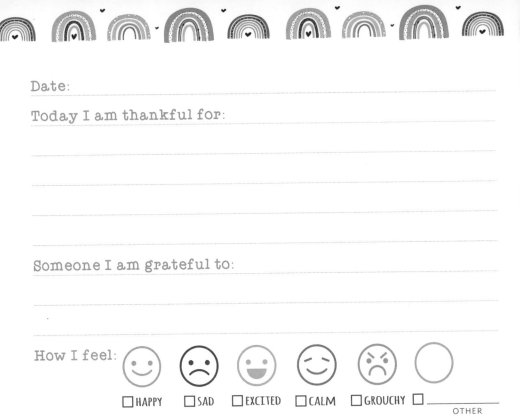

Date:

Today I am thankful for:

Someone I am grateful to:

How I feel:

☐ HAPPY ☐ SAD ☐ EXCITED ☐ CALM ☐ GROUCHY ☐ _____ OTHER

The BEST part of my day (draw and/or write about it):

Date:

Today I am thankful for:

Someone I am grateful to:

How I feel: ☐ HAPPY ☐ SAD ☐ EXCITED ☐ CALM ☐ GROUCHY ☐ _____
OTHER

The BEST part of my day (draw and/or write about it):

Date:

Today I am thankful for:

Someone I am grateful to:

How I feel: ☺ ☹ 😀 😌 😠 ○

☐ HAPPY ☐ SAD ☐ EXCITED ☐ CALM ☐ GROUCHY ☐ _____ OTHER

The BEST part of my day (draw and/or write about it):

Weekly Acts of
Kindness

How I showed kindness this week:

_____

_____

_____

_____

_____

_____

What I'm looking forward to next week:

_____

_____

_____

_____

_____

_____

Courage. Kindness. Friendship. Character.
These are the qualities that define us as human
beings, and propel us, on occasion, to greatness.

— R. J. PALACIO, *WONDER*

Date:

Today I am thankful for:

Someone I am grateful to:

How I feel:

☐ HAPPY ☐ SAD ☐ EXCITED ☐ CALM ☐ GROUCHY ☐ _____
OTHER

The **BEST** part of my day (draw and/or write about it):

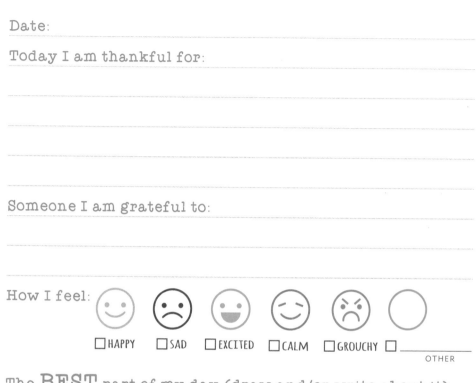

Date:

Today I am thankful for:

Someone I am grateful to:

How I feel:
☐ HAPPY ☐ SAD ☐ EXCITED ☐ CALM ☐ GROUCHY ☐ _____
OTHER

The **BEST** part of my day (draw and/or write about it):

Date:

Today I am thankful for:

Someone I am grateful to:

How I feel:

☐ HAPPY ☐ SAD ☐ EXCITED ☐ CALM ☐ GROUCHY ☐ _____
                                                        OTHER

The **BEST** part of my day (draw and/or write about it):

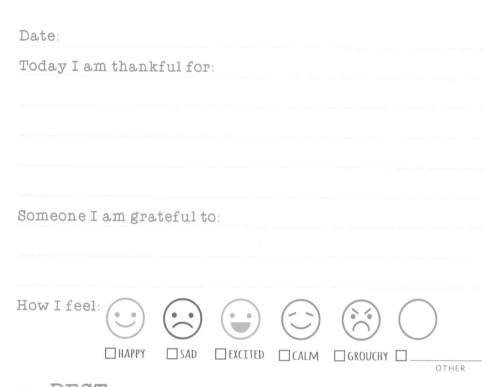

Date:

Today I am thankful for:

Someone I am grateful to:

How I feel:

☐ HAPPY ☐ SAD ☐ EXCITED ☐ CALM ☐ GROUCHY ☐ _____
                                                        OTHER

The BEST part of my day (draw and/or write about it):

Date:

Today I am thankful for:

Someone I am grateful to:

How I feel:

☐ HAPPY   ☐ SAD   ☐ EXCITED   ☐ CALM   ☐ GROUCHY   ☐ _____
OTHER

The **BEST** part of my day (draw and/or write about it):

Date:

Today I am thankful for:

Someone I am grateful to:

How I feel:

☐ HAPPY ☐ SAD ☐ EXCITED ☐ CALM ☐ GROUCHY ☐ _____

OTHER

The **BEST** part of my day (draw and/or write about it):

Date: ....

Today I am thankful for: ....

....

....

....

....

Someone I am grateful to: ....

....

....

How I feel:

☐ HAPPY　　☐ SAD　　☐ EXCITED　　☐ CALM　　☐ GROUCHY　　☐ _____
　　　　　　　　　　　　　　　　　　　　　　　　　　　　　　　　　　OTHER

The BEST part of my day (draw and/or write about it):

Weekly Acts of
Kindness

How I showed kindness this week:

_____

_____

_____

_____

_____

What I'm looking forward to next week:

_____

_____

_____

_____

_____

This is a wonderful day.
I've never seen this one before.

— MAYA ANGELOU

Date:

Today I am thankful for:

Someone I am grateful to:

How I feel:

☐ HAPPY ☐ SAD ☐ EXCITED ☐ CALM ☐ GROUCHY ☐ _____
OTHER

The **BEST** part of my day (draw and/or write about it):

Date:

Today I am thankful for:

Someone I am grateful to:

How I feel:

☐ HAPPY   ☐ SAD   ☐ EXCITED   ☐ CALM   ☐ GROUCHY   ☐ _____
OTHER

The BEST part of my day (draw and/or write about it):

Date:

Today I am thankful for:

Someone I am grateful to:

How I feel:

☐ HAPPY ☐ SAD ☐ EXCITED ☐ CALM ☐ GROUCHY ☐ _____
OTHER

The BEST part of my day (draw and/or write about it):

Date:

Today I am thankful for:

Someone I am grateful to:

How I feel:

☐ HAPPY ☐ SAD ☐ EXCITED ☐ CALM ☐ GROUCHY ☐ _____
OTHER

The **BEST** part of my day (draw and/or write about it):

Date:

Today I am thankful for:

Someone I am grateful to:

How I feel:

☐ HAPPY ☐ SAD ☐ EXCITED ☐ CALM ☐ GROUCHY ☐ _____
OTHER

The BEST part of my day (draw and/or write about it):

Date:

Today I am thankful for:

Someone I am grateful to:

How I feel:

☐ HAPPY ☐ SAD ☐ EXCITED ☐ CALM ☐ GROUCHY ☐ _____
OTHER

The BEST part of my day (draw and/or write about it):

Date:

Today I am thankful for:

Someone I am grateful to:

How I feel:

☐ HAPPY ☐ SAD ☐ EXCITED ☐ CALM ☐ GROUCHY ☐ _____
                                                          OTHER

The BEST part of my day (draw and/or write about it):

Weekly Acts of
Kindness

How I showed kindness this week:

_____

_____

_____

_____

_____

What I'm looking forward to next week:

_____

_____

_____

_____

Those who bring sunshine into
the lives of others cannot keep
it from themselves.

– J. M. BARRIE

Date:

Today I am thankful for:

Someone I am grateful to:

How I feel: ☺ ☹ 😀 😌 😠 ◯

☐ HAPPY ☐ SAD ☐ EXCITED ☐ CALM ☐ GROUCHY ☐ _____
OTHER

The **BEST** part of my day (draw and/or write about it):

Date:

Today I am thankful for:

Someone I am grateful to:

How I feel:

☐ HAPPY ☐ SAD ☐ EXCITED ☐ CALM ☐ GROUCHY ☐ _____
OTHER

The BEST part of my day (draw and/or write about it):

Date: _____

Today I am thankful for:
_____
_____
_____

Someone I am grateful to:
_____
_____

How I feel:

☐ HAPPY ☐ SAD ☐ EXCITED ☐ CALM ☐ GROUCHY ☐ _____ OTHER

The BEST part of my day (draw and/or write about it):

Date:

Today I am thankful for:

Someone I am grateful to:

How I feel:

☐ HAPPY ☐ SAD ☐ EXCITED ☐ CALM ☐ GROUCHY ☐ _____
OTHER

The BEST part of my day (draw and/or write about it):

Date: ....

Today I am thankful for: ....

....

....

....

....

Someone I am grateful to: ....

....

How I feel:

☐ HAPPY ☐ SAD ☐ EXCITED ☐ CALM ☐ GROUCHY ☐ _____
OTHER

The BEST part of my day (draw and/or write about it):

Date:

Today I am thankful for:

Someone I am grateful to:

How I feel:

☐ HAPPY ☐ SAD ☐ EXCITED ☐ CALM ☐ GROUCHY ☐ _____
OTHER

The BEST part of my day (draw and/or write about it):

Date:
....

Today I am thankful for:
....

....

....

....

Someone I am grateful to:
....

....

How I feel:

☐ HAPPY ☐ SAD ☐ EXCITED ☐ CALM ☐ GROUCHY ☐ _____ OTHER

The BEST part of my day (draw and/or write about it):

Weekly Acts of
Kindness

How I showed kindness this week:

What I'm looking forward to next week:

Date:

Today I am thankful for:

Someone I am grateful to:

How I feel:

☐ HAPPY ☐ SAD ☐ EXCITED ☐ CALM ☐ GROUCHY ☐ _____
                                                      OTHER

The **BEST** part of my day (draw and/or write about it):

Date: _____

Today I am thankful for: _____

_____

_____

_____

Someone I am grateful to: _____

_____

How I feel: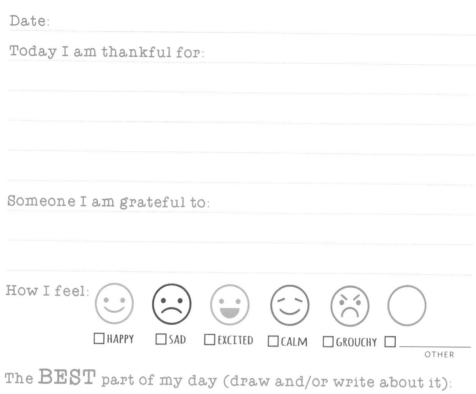

☐ HAPPY   ☐ SAD   ☐ EXCITED   ☐ CALM   ☐ GROUCHY   ☐ _____

OTHER

The BEST part of my day (draw and/or write about it):

Date: _____

Today I am thankful for: _____

_____

_____

_____

Someone I am grateful to: _____

_____

_____

How I feel:

☐ HAPPY   ☐ SAD   ☐ EXCITED   ☐ CALM   ☐ GROUCHY   ☐ _____
                                                                    OTHER

The **BEST** part of my day (draw and/or write about it):

Date:

Today I am thankful for:

Someone I am grateful to:

How I feel:

☐ HAPPY   ☐ SAD   ☐ EXCITED   ☐ CALM   ☐ GROUCHY   ☐ _____
OTHER

The **BEST** part of my day (draw and/or write about it):

Date:

Today I am thankful for:

Someone I am grateful to:

How I feel:

☐ HAPPY ☐ SAD ☐ EXCITED ☐ CALM ☐ GROUCHY ☐ _____
OTHER

The BEST part of my day (draw and/or write about it):

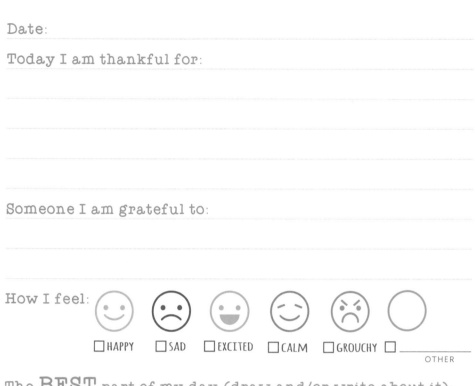

Date:

Today I am thankful for:

Someone I am grateful to:

How I feel:

☐ HAPPY   ☐ SAD   ☐ EXCITED   ☐ CALM   ☐ GROUCHY   ☐ _____
OTHER

The BEST part of my day (draw and/or write about it):

Date: _____

Today I am thankful for: _____

_____

_____

_____

Someone I am grateful to: _____

_____

_____

How I feel:

☐ HAPPY   ☐ SAD   ☐ EXCITED   ☐ CALM   ☐ GROUCHY   ☐ _____
OTHER

The BEST part of my day (draw and/or write about it):

Weekly Acts of
Kindness

How I showed kindness this week:

_____

_____

_____

_____

_____

What I'm looking forward to next week:

_____

_____

_____

_____

_____

If you have good thoughts they will
shine out of your face like sunbeams
and you will always look lovely.

— ROALD DAHL

Date: ....

Today I am thankful for: ....

....

....

....

....

Someone I am grateful to: ....

....

....

How I feel:

☐ HAPPY   ☐ SAD   ☐ EXCITED   ☐ CALM   ☐ GROUCHY   ☐ _____ OTHER

The **BEST** part of my day (draw and/or write about it):

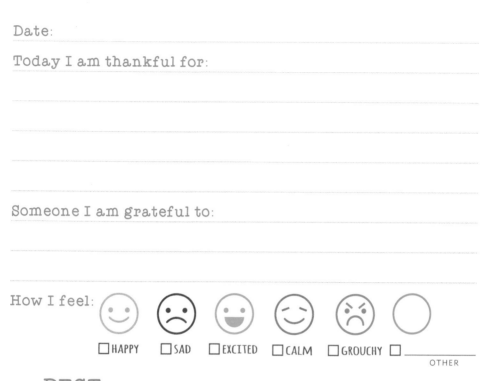

Date:

Today I am thankful for:

Someone I am grateful to:

How I feel:

☐ HAPPY ☐ SAD ☐ EXCITED ☐ CALM ☐ GROUCHY ☐ _____
OTHER

The BEST part of my day (draw and/or write about it):

Date:

Today I am thankful for:

Someone I am grateful to:

How I feel:

☐ HAPPY ☐ SAD ☐ EXCITED ☐ CALM ☐ GROUCHY ☐ _____
OTHER

The BEST part of my day (draw and/or write about it):

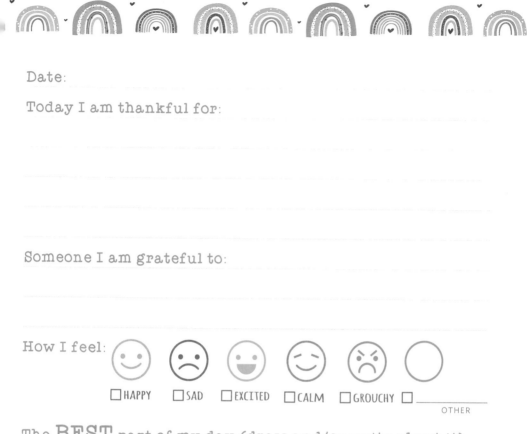

Date:

Today I am thankful for:

Someone I am grateful to:

How I feel:

☐ HAPPY ☐ SAD ☐ EXCITED ☐ CALM ☐ GROUCHY ☐ _____
                                                              OTHER

The BEST part of my day (draw and/or write about it):

Date: ....

Today I am thankful for: ....

....

....

....

....

Someone I am grateful to: ....

....

....

How I feel:

☐ HAPPY   ☐ SAD   ☐ EXCITED   ☐ CALM   ☐ GROUCHY   ☐ _____
OTHER

The **BEST** part of my day (draw and/or write about it):

Date:

Today I am thankful for:

Someone I am grateful to:

How I feel:

☐ HAPPY   ☐ SAD   ☐ EXCITED   ☐ CALM   ☐ GROUCHY   ☐ _____
OTHER

The BEST part of my day (draw and/or write about it):

Date:

Today I am thankful for:

Someone I am grateful to:

How I feel:

☐ HAPPY ☐ SAD ☐ EXCITED ☐ CALM ☐ GROUCHY ☐ _____
OTHER

The BEST part of my day (draw and/or write about it):

Weekly Acts of
Kindness

How I showed kindness this week:

_____

_____

_____

_____

_____

_____

What I'm looking forward to next week:

_____

_____

_____

_____

_____

_____

Never believe that a few caring
people can't change the world.
For indeed that's all who ever have.

— MARGARET MEAD

Date:

Today I am thankful for:

Someone I am grateful to:

How I feel:

☐ HAPPY   ☐ SAD   ☐ EXCITED   ☐ CALM   ☐ GROUCHY   ☐ _____
OTHER

The **BEST** part of my day (draw and/or write about it):

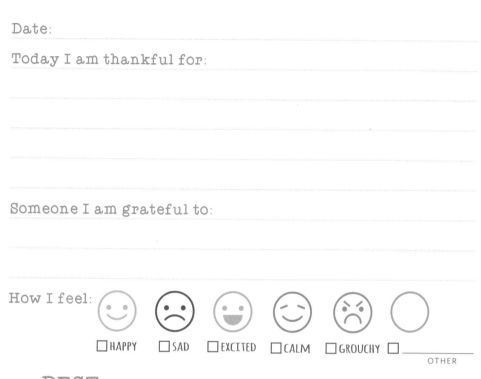

Date:

Today I am thankful for:

Someone I am grateful to:

How I feel:

☐ HAPPY   ☐ SAD   ☐ EXCITED   ☐ CALM   ☐ GROUCHY   ☐ _____
OTHER

The **BEST** part of my day (draw and/or write about it):

Date:

Today I am thankful for:

Someone I am grateful to:

How I feel:

☐ HAPPY ☐ SAD ☐ EXCITED ☐ CALM ☐ GROUCHY ☐ _____
OTHER

The BEST part of my day (draw and/or write about it):

Date:

Today I am thankful for:

Someone I am grateful to:

How I feel:

☐ HAPPY ☐ SAD ☐ EXCITED ☐ CALM ☐ GROUCHY ☐ _____
OTHER

The BEST part of my day (draw and/or write about it):

Date: ....

Today I am thankful for: ....

....

....

....

Someone I am grateful to: ....

....

How I feel:

☐ HAPPY   ☐ SAD   ☐ EXCITED   ☐ CALM   ☐ GROUCHY   ☐ _____
OTHER

The BEST part of my day (draw and/or write about it):

Date:

Today I am thankful for:

Someone I am grateful to:

How I feel:

☐ HAPPY ☐ SAD ☐ EXCITED ☐ CALM ☐ GROUCHY ☐ _____
OTHER

The BEST part of my day (draw and/or write about it):

Date: _____

Today I am thankful for:

_____

_____

_____

_____

Someone I am grateful to: _____

_____

How I feel:

☐ HAPPY   ☐ SAD   ☐ EXCITED   ☐ CALM   ☐ GROUCHY   ☐ _____
OTHER

The **BEST** part of my day (draw and/or write about it):

Weekly Acts of Kindness

How I showed kindness this week:

What I'm looking forward to next week:

How much good inside a day?
Depends how good you live 'em.

– SHEL SILVERSTEIN, *A LIGHT IN THE ATTIC*

Date:

Today I am thankful for:

Someone I am grateful to:

How I feel:

☐ HAPPY   ☐ SAD   ☐ EXCITED   ☐ CALM   ☐ GROUCHY   ☐ _____
                                                          OTHER

The **BEST** part of my day (draw and/or write about it):

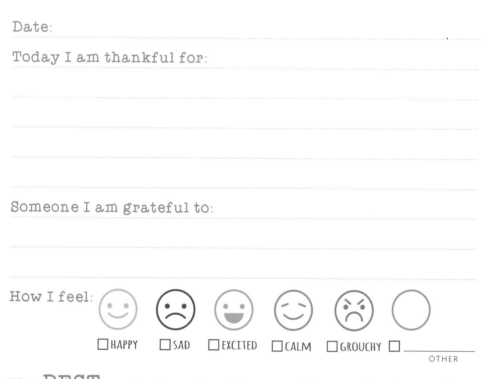

Date:

Today I am thankful for:

Someone I am grateful to:

How I feel:

☐ HAPPY ☐ SAD ☐ EXCITED ☐ CALM ☐ GROUCHY ☐ _____
OTHER

The **BEST** part of my day (draw and/or write about it):

Date:

Today I am thankful for:

Someone I am grateful to:

How I feel:

☐ HAPPY   ☐ SAD   ☐ EXCITED   ☐ CALM   ☐ GROUCHY   ☐ _____
OTHER

The BEST part of my day (draw and/or write about it):

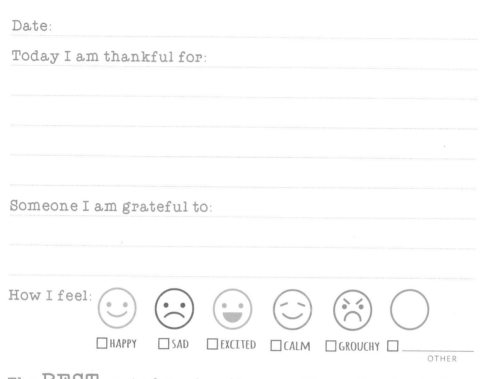

Date:

Today I am thankful for:

Someone I am grateful to:

How I feel:

☐ HAPPY   ☐ SAD   ☐ EXCITED   ☐ CALM   ☐ GROUCHY   ☐ _____
                                                              OTHER

The BEST part of my day (draw and/or write about it):

Date:

Today I am thankful for:

Someone I am grateful to:

How I feel:

☐ HAPPY ☐ SAD ☐ EXCITED ☐ CALM ☐ GROUCHY ☐ _____ OTHER

The BEST part of my day (draw and/or write about it):

Date:

Today I am thankful for:

Someone I am grateful to:

How I feel:

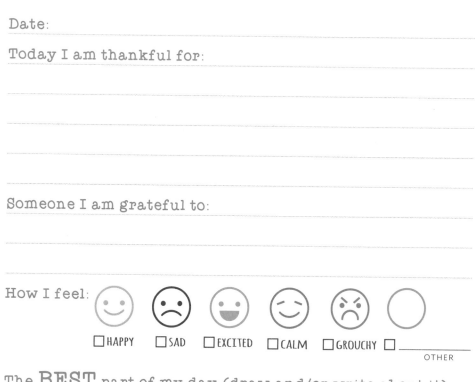

☐ HAPPY ☐ SAD ☐ EXCITED ☐ CALM ☐ GROUCHY ☐ _____
OTHER

The BEST part of my day (draw and/or write about it):

Date: ....

Today I am thankful for: ....

....

....

....

....

Someone I am grateful to: ....

....

....

How I feel:

☐ HAPPY   ☐ SAD   ☐ EXCITED   ☐ CALM   ☐ GROUCHY   ☐ _____
OTHER

The BEST part of my day (draw and/or write about it):

Weekly Acts of Kindness

How I showed kindness this week:

What I'm looking forward to next week:

*If you want to find happiness,
find gratitude.*

— STEVE MARABOLI

Date:

Today I am thankful for:

Someone I am grateful to:

How I feel:

☐ HAPPY ☐ SAD ☐ EXCITED ☐ CALM ☐ GROUCHY ☐ _____ OTHER

The BEST part of my day (draw and/or write about it):

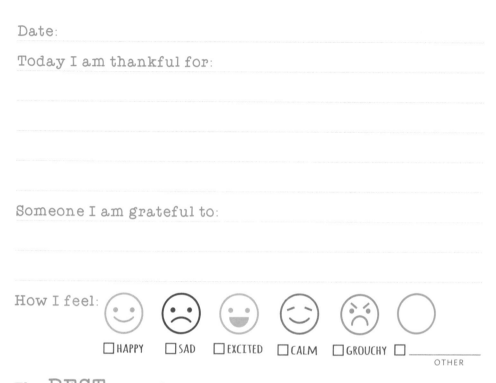

Date:

Today I am thankful for:

Someone I am grateful to:

How I feel:

☐ HAPPY ☐ SAD ☐ EXCITED ☐ CALM ☐ GROUCHY ☐ _____
OTHER

The **BEST** part of my day (draw and/or write about it):

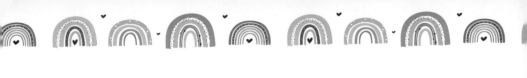

Date:

Today I am thankful for:

Someone I am grateful to:

How I feel:

☐ HAPPY ☐ SAD ☐ EXCITED ☐ CALM ☐ GROUCHY ☐ _____
OTHER

The BEST part of my day (draw and/or write about it):

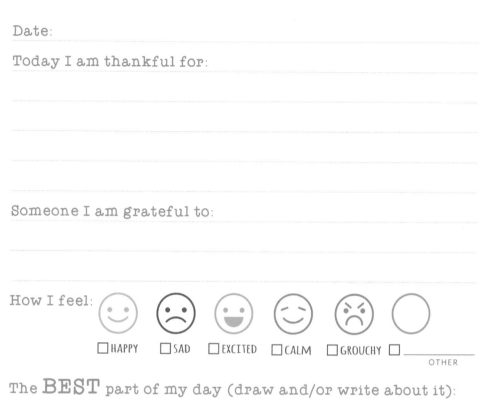

Date:

Today I am thankful for:

Someone I am grateful to:

How I feel: ☐ HAPPY ☐ SAD ☐ EXCITED ☐ CALM ☐ GROUCHY ☐ _____ OTHER

The BEST part of my day (draw and/or write about it):

Date:

Today I am thankful for:

Someone I am grateful to:

How I feel:

☐ HAPPY ☐ SAD ☐ EXCITED ☐ CALM ☐ GROUCHY ☐ _____
OTHER

The BEST part of my day (draw and/or write about it):

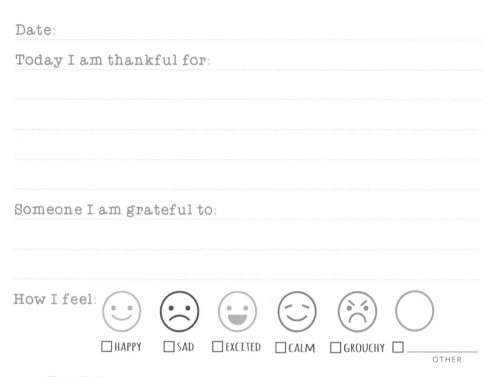

Date:

Today I am thankful for:

Someone I am grateful to:

How I feel:

☐ HAPPY ☐ SAD ☐ EXCITED ☐ CALM ☐ GROUCHY ☐ _____
OTHER

The **BEST** part of my day (draw and/or write about it):

Date: ....

Today I am thankful for: ....

....

....

....

....

Someone I am grateful to: ....

....

....

How I feel: ☺ ☹ 😀 😌 😠 ○

☐ HAPPY   ☐ SAD   ☐ EXCITED   ☐ CALM   ☐ GROUCHY   ☐ _____
OTHER

The BEST part of my day (draw and/or write about it):

Weekly Acts of Kindness

How I showed kindness this week:

_____

_____

_____

_____

_____

What I'm looking forward to next week:

_____

_____

_____

_____

_____

Sometimes the smallest things take
up the most room in your heart.

— A .A. MILNE, *WINNIE-THE-POOH*

Date: ....

Today I am thankful for: ....

....

....

....

....

Someone I am grateful to: ....

....

....

How I feel:

☐ HAPPY   ☐ SAD   ☐ EXCITED   ☐ CALM   ☐ GROUCHY   ☐ _____
OTHER

The BEST part of my day (draw and/or write about it):

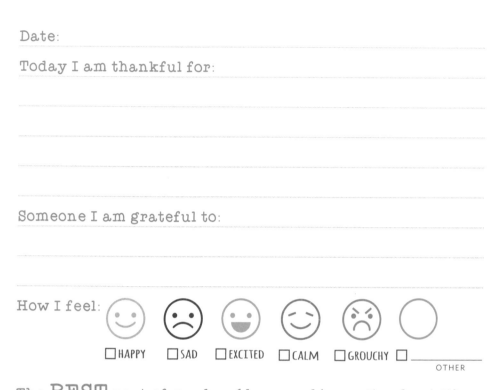

Date:

Today I am thankful for:

Someone I am grateful to:

How I feel:

☐ HAPPY ☐ SAD ☐ EXCITED ☐ CALM ☐ GROUCHY ☐ _____
OTHER

The BEST part of my day (draw and/or write about it):

Date: ....

Today I am thankful for: ....

....

....

....

....

Someone I am grateful to: ....

....

....

How I feel:

☐ HAPPY   ☐ SAD   ☐ EXCITED   ☐ CALM   ☐ GROUCHY   ☐ _____
OTHER

The BEST part of my day (draw and/or write about it):

Date:

Today I am thankful for:

Someone I am grateful to:

How I feel:

☐ HAPPY ☐ SAD ☐ EXCITED ☐ CALM ☐ GROUCHY ☐ _____
OTHER

The BEST part of my day (draw and/or write about it):

Date:

Today I am thankful for:

Someone I am grateful to:

How I feel:

☐ HAPPY   ☐ SAD   ☐ EXCITED   ☐ CALM   ☐ GROUCHY   ☐ _____
OTHER

The **BEST** part of my day (draw and/or write about it):

Date:

Today I am thankful for:

Someone I am grateful to:

How I feel:

☐ HAPPY   ☐ SAD   ☐ EXCITED   ☐ CALM   ☐ GROUCHY   ☐ _____
OTHER

The BEST part of my day (draw and/or write about it):

Date:

Today I am thankful for:

Someone I am grateful to:

How I feel:

☐ HAPPY ☐ SAD ☐ EXCITED ☐ CALM ☐ GROUCHY ☐ _____ OTHER

The BEST part of my day (draw and/or write about it):

Weekly Acts of Kindness

How I showed kindness this week:

What I'm looking forward to next week:

It is in your hands to make our
world a better one for all.

— NELSON MANDELA

Date:

Today I am thankful for:

Someone I am grateful to:

How I feel: ☺ ☹ 😃 ☺ 😠 ○

☐ HAPPY ☐ SAD ☐ EXCITED ☐ CALM ☐ GROUCHY ☐ _____
OTHER

The **BEST** part of my day (draw and/or write about it):

Date:

Today I am thankful for:

Someone I am grateful to:

How I feel:

☐ HAPPY ☐ SAD ☐ EXCITED ☐ CALM ☐ GROUCHY ☐ _____
OTHER

The BEST part of my day (draw and/or write about it):

Date: _____

Today I am thankful for: _____

_____

_____

_____

Someone I am grateful to: _____

_____

How I feel: 😊 😞 😁 😌 😠 ◯

☐ HAPPY ☐ SAD ☐ EXCITED ☐ CALM ☐ GROUCHY ☐ _____ OTHER

The BEST part of my day (draw and/or write about it):

Date:

Today I am thankful for:

Someone I am grateful to:

How I feel:

☐ HAPPY   ☐ SAD   ☐ EXCITED   ☐ CALM   ☐ GROUCHY   ☐ _____
OTHER

The BEST part of my day (draw and/or write about it):

Date:

Today I am thankful for:

Someone I am grateful to:

How I feel: ☐ HAPPY ☐ SAD ☐ EXCITED ☐ CALM ☐ GROUCHY ☐ _____
                                                                        OTHER

The BEST part of my day (draw and/or write about it):

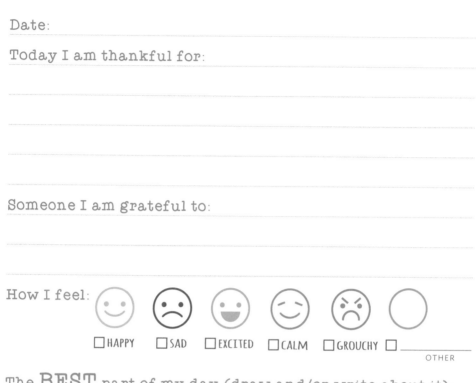

Date:

Today I am thankful for:

Someone I am grateful to:

How I feel:

☐ HAPPY ☐ SAD ☐ EXCITED ☐ CALM ☐ GROUCHY ☐ _____
OTHER

The **BEST** part of my day (draw and/or write about it):

Date:

Today I am thankful for:

Someone I am grateful to:

How I feel:

☐ HAPPY ☐ SAD ☐ EXCITED ☐ CALM ☐ GROUCHY ☐ _____ OTHER

The BEST part of my day (draw and/or write about it):

Weekly Acts of Kindness

How I showed kindness this week:

What I'm looking forward to next week:

My town is called *Who*-ville, for I am a *Who*
And we *Whos* are all thankful
and grateful to you.

— DR. SEUSS, *HORTON HEARS A WHO*

Date:

Today I am thankful for:

Someone I am grateful to:

How I feel:

☐ HAPPY   ☐ SAD   ☐ EXCITED   ☐ CALM   ☐ GROUCHY   ☐ _____
OTHER

The **BEST** part of my day (draw and/or write about it):

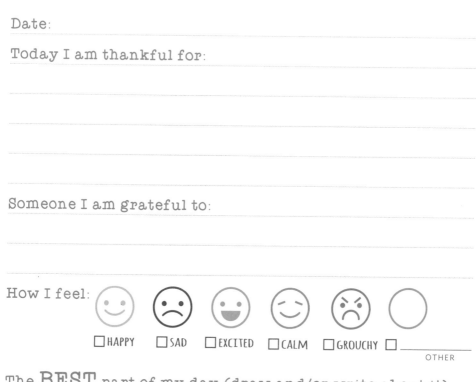

Date:

Today I am thankful for:

Someone I am grateful to:

How I feel:

☐ HAPPY ☐ SAD ☐ EXCITED ☐ CALM ☐ GROUCHY ☐ _____
OTHER

The BEST part of my day (draw and/or write about it):

Date: _____

Today I am thankful for: _____

_____

_____

_____

Someone I am grateful to: _____

_____

How I feel:

☐ HAPPY   ☐ SAD   ☐ EXCITED   ☐ CALM   ☐ GROUCHY   ☐ _____
OTHER

The **BEST** part of my day (draw and/or write about it):

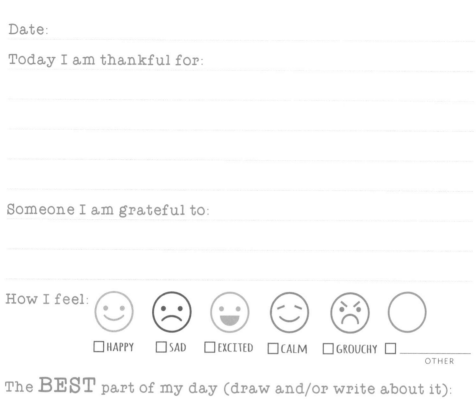

Date:

Today I am thankful for:

Someone I am grateful to:

How I feel:

☐ HAPPY   ☐ SAD   ☐ EXCITED   ☐ CALM   ☐ GROUCHY   ☐ _____
                                                              OTHER

The BEST part of my day (draw and/or write about it):

Date:

Today I am thankful for:

Someone I am grateful to:

How I feel:

☐ HAPPY ☐ SAD ☐ EXCITED ☐ CALM ☐ GROUCHY ☐ _____ OTHER

The BEST part of my day (draw and/or write about it):

Date:

Today I am thankful for:

Someone I am grateful to:

How I feel:

☐ HAPPY ☐ SAD ☐ EXCITED ☐ CALM ☐ GROUCHY ☐ _____
OTHER

The BEST part of my day (draw and/or write about it):

Date: ....

Today I am thankful for: ....

....

....

....

....

Someone I am grateful to: ....

....

How I feel:

☐ HAPPY ☐ SAD ☐ EXCITED ☐ CALM ☐ GROUCHY ☐ _____
OTHER

The BEST part of my day (draw and/or write about it):

Weekly Acts of Kindness

How I showed kindness this week:

What I'm looking forward to next week:

We can complain because rose bushes
have thorns, or rejoice because
thorns have roses.

— ALPHONSE KARR, *A TOUR ROUND MY GARDEN*

Date:

Today I am thankful for:

Someone I am grateful to:

How I feel:

☐ HAPPY ☐ SAD ☐ EXCITED ☐ CALM ☐ GROUCHY ☐ _____ OTHER

The **BEST** part of my day (draw and/or write about it):

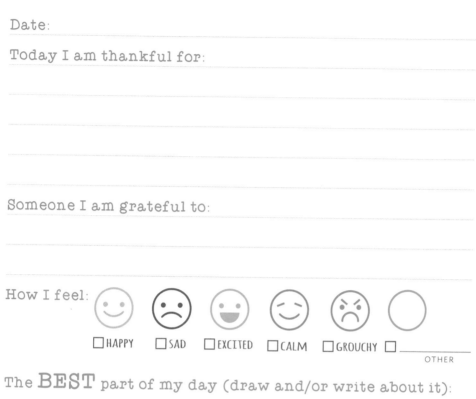

Date:

Today I am thankful for:

Someone I am grateful to:

How I feel:

☐ HAPPY   ☐ SAD   ☐ EXCITED   ☐ CALM   ☐ GROUCHY   ☐ _____
OTHER

The **BEST** part of my day (draw and/or write about it):

Date:

Today I am thankful for:

Someone I am grateful to:

How I feel:

☐ HAPPY ☐ SAD ☐ EXCITED ☐ CALM ☐ GROUCHY ☐ _____
OTHER

The **BEST** part of my day (draw and/or write about it):

Date:

Today I am thankful for:

Someone I am grateful to:

How I feel:

☐ HAPPY ☐ SAD ☐ EXCITED ☐ CALM ☐ GROUCHY ☐ _____
OTHER

The BEST part of my day (draw and/or write about it):

Date:

Today I am thankful for:

Someone I am grateful to:

How I feel:

☐ HAPPY   ☐ SAD   ☐ EXCITED   ☐ CALM   ☐ GROUCHY   ☐ _____
OTHER

The BEST part of my day (draw and/or write about it):

Date:

Today I am thankful for:

Someone I am grateful to:

How I feel: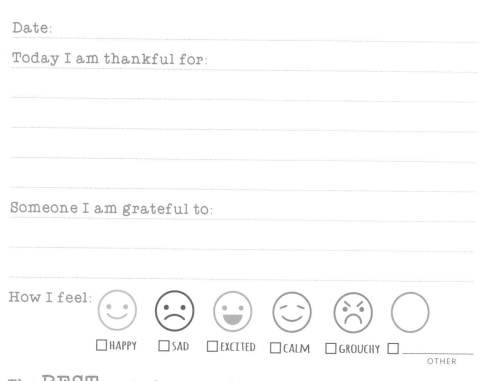

☐ HAPPY ☐ SAD ☐ EXCITED ☐ CALM ☐ GROUCHY ☐ _____
OTHER

The BEST part of my day (draw and/or write about it):

Date: _____

Today I am thankful for: _____

_____

_____

_____

_____

Someone I am grateful to: _____

_____

_____

How I feel:

☐ HAPPY ☐ SAD ☐ EXCITED ☐ CALM ☐ GROUCHY ☐ _____
                                                      OTHER

The BEST part of my day (draw and/or write about it):

Weekly Acts of
Kindness

How I showed kindness this week:

_____

_____

_____

_____

_____

What I'm looking forward to next week:

_____

_____

_____

_____

No act of kindness, no matter
how small, is ever wasted.

– AESOP

Gratitude in Action

Here are a few examples to get you started:

- Write a thank-you note to a friend, relative, teacher, or someone in your community.
- Make a gift for someone you care about.
- Write positive messages on the sidewalk with chalk.
- Tell everyone in your family what you love about them.
- Donate or pass on old toys, books, and clothes.
- **Pitch in around the house (without being asked).**
- Be a study buddy with someone at school—or help a sibling with homework.
- Paint rocks with kind words and put them around your neighborhood for others to find.
- Recycle and reuse—help our planet!
- Call a grandparent or relative and ask how they are doing.

Those who are happiest are those who do the most for others.

— BOOKER T. WASHINGTON

Be Grateful
and
Kind

Piglet noticed that even though
he had a very small heart,
it could hold a rather
large amount of gratitude.

- A. A. MILNE, *WINNIE-THE-POOH*